Pillars

of

Excellence

Adrian Taylor, Jr.

The Apostle of Truth

Adrian Taylor, Jr.

Unattributed quotations are by Beatrice Bruno

Unless otherwise indicated, Scripture quotations are from the King James Version of the Holy Bible.

Published by Heard Word Publishing, LLC
1980 Van Buren Way
Aurora, CO 0011

ISBN: 0-9801060-2-8

ISBN-13: 978-0-9801060-2-2

Copies of *Pillars of Excellence* and other books by Adrian Taylor, Jr. are available at http://drillsergeantoflife.com/heard-word-publishing/.

Adrian Taylor, Jr.

DEDICATION

This book is dedicated to the one *thing* most responsible for helping me learn the principles taught in these pages. That *thing* of which I speak is my "***Good Thing***" from the Lord – my wife,

LaKenya LaVonna Taylor.

Thank you for always being truthful with me and honest before God. If ever there was a woman who loved God, you are her. I love you more now than ever and I'll love you more tomorrow than today.

Proverbs 18:22 *Whoso findeth a wife findeth a good thing, and obtaineth favour of the Lord.*

Adrian Taylor, Jr.

Here's what people are saying about

Pillars of Excellence:

"With fervor, Adrian Taylor, Jr. writes to inspire the Body of Christ to cease settling for a mediocre existence and to rise to excellence in every area of life. Using memorable illustrations, Taylor presents several "*pillars*" which, when habituated, exhibits the excellence of God in families, communities, businesses and government. Implementing the principles set forth in *Pillars of Excellence* can motivate the reader to actualize the abundant life God intended for His people."

Dr. Dorothy J. Haire, BS, MA, MTh, DMin.
Pastor, Teacher, Speaker, Writer

"Like a voice crying in the wilderness, Apostle Adrian Taylor, Jr. calls us back to the basic fundamentals necessary to build a productive, God-honoring life, church, organization, or society. If you desire more than mediocrity in your life, clear your schedule, find a quiet spot, and pull up a chair with this book. *Pillars of Excellence* will challenge you, convict you, and point you down the path that leads to significance!"

Chris Vaught
Pastor, Speaker, Author

"In *Pillars of Excellence,* Apostle Adrian Taylor, Jr. very eloquently brings **Excellence** to the focal point! Apostle Taylor lays out the road map for us to take back what the devil has stolen! He points out pertinent changes that *must* be made so that the Church, the Body of Christ, can ascend to the high level of excellence again.

Pillars of Excellence sows seeds of excellence into your life causing an abundant harvest to come forth. Excellence lifts you up and out of every valley you may currently dwell in. God's excellent breath breathes on all the dry bones in your life. As you read *Pillars of Excellence*, God is raising an *Army of Excellence* in which you are included!"

God bless you all!

Pastor Tyronne Stowe
Gospel 4 Life Church
Chandler AZ

"**This book is tremendous!** *Pillars of Excellence* defines the excellence of the foundation and function of a person in the Body of Christ and the Kingdom of God. I believe every leader and every individual, regardless of their various levels of success but who are reaching to achieve higher levels in God, should read *Pillars of Excellence.*"

Pastor Taylor, may your book touch and move the hearts of God's people. Bless you!

Pastor Zack Strong
Christ Church of the Heartland
Cape Girardeau, MO 63701

"When surrounded with mediocrity, excellence stands out as a beacon of light. The problem we face is the progressive and almost subtle decline of our standards because of that mediocrity. By lacking excellence, we begin living casually, then carelessly, then recklessly. Pastor Adrian Taylor has challenged us to raise our bar higher with *"Pillars of Excellence."*

If you are tired of settling for second best or just being average, let this book stir you to be all God expects you to be. Then, allow the practical and biblical wisdom of this book to create new *"Pillars of Excellence"* in your life."

Pastor Michael A. Ware
Victory Church – Denver

CONTENTS

Adrian Taylor, Jr.

FOREWORD

The 21st Century New Testament Messianic Church of the Lord Jesus Christ is faced with some great challenges. In our society, these challenges war against the very core of God's standard righteousness for His chosen and covenant people. These challenges are designed to pressure the Church - the Community of believers in Christ - to become tolerant and to compromise God's standard of righteousness. Doing so only accommodates and pleases the carnal and untamed fleshly, greedy, and never-satisfied lusts of men.

Are there any prophets and people of God who refuse to bow their hearts and knees to the Baal of our day? Are there any who will remain loyal and true to the LORD their God?

We have found such a prophet in Adrian Taylor, Jr. An Apostle, called by God for such a time as this, Adrian has written **Pillars of Excellence,** a book that will challenge every church, shepherd and believer. It will challenge all who read each precious page to examine hearts, lives and motives to see whether we are bowing and compromising or remaining loyal and steadfast. The times we currently live in are so critical to the righteousness of God. His followers are to boldly demonstrate as His representatives in the earth.

Adrian's book, **Pillars of Excellence**, is very timely, seasonal, and enlightening. You can feel his sincere heart and concern as you read, study, and meditate upon each word. Although Adrian deals with topics or subjects we have heard and studied before, in **Pillars of Excellence,** he is merely putting us in remembrance of what we have a tendency of getting slack in. And, sometimes, just neglect. And, he does it in a very refreshing and welcoming way.

The very foundation and infrastructure of the righteousness of God, the standard He has set and established for those whom He has declared righteous on the basis of their faith in Jesus Christ is being compromised! The adversary and enemies of Christ and the Cross even attempt to demolish the **high standards** of Adonai to His displeasure in order to establish and embrace the *low standard* of men to their pleasure and delight. This is being done by those professing to be believers and a part of the *true* Church of Jesus Christ.

A well-known pastor of a large church in the South recently stated, *"We must adjust the Church to fit and accommodate the culture of the 21st Century."*

Since when has God told His people to listen to the world and this evil generation and allow them to tell us what we should believe, how we should live, what's holy, and what standard we should live by? God sets the standard and the standard has already been uncompromisingly set! The very day the Church seeks to please men in order to satisfy their unbridled, unsatisfied lusts and affections, and abandons the standard of God's righteousness, good deeds, and morality (**which cannot be legislated!**) is the very day we *cease* pleasing the LORD Who has called and saved us.

Prepare to be challenged, convicted, changed and consecrated again to the righteousness of God, wholly and without compromise, as you read *Pillars of Excellence*!

Someone has said, "*Excellence is not a place we finally arrive at and attain. It simply means that you keep getting better at what you were called to be and to do.*"

Let us all examine, study, and apply the *pillars* in this book. Let us allow Christ to build His Church in such a way that we will be erected and established and well-able to stand uncompromisingly in the truth and righteousness of the LORD, being full of the love and compassion of the Lord in our hearts.

Great Book!

Dr. Maurice K. Wright, Th. D.
United Christian Church
Gadsden, Alabama

PREFACE

In this post-modern society, it has become commonplace to accept a declining bar of mediocrity as the status quo. There was a time when people displayed a sense of decency in honoring and respecting others.

In the not-so-distant past, business owners took great care in servicing their patrons. They wanted their customers to know that their business was wanted and appreciated. Business contracts were sealed with a smile and a firm handshake. A person meant what he said and could be trusted to do exactly what he said.

The value of people has diminished. It has been replaced with the bottom line: *money at any cost.* This new mantra has become the order of the day and the *exceptional* has been replaced by the *unthinkable*.

Big corporations have all but removed the small business owner. They are getting larger but the quality of their products does not match their size. A simple stroll through the nearest supermarket reveals this fact.

The price of a loaf of bread increases while the size of that same loaf shrinks. Fast food restaurants advertise massive sandwiches and drinks. However, once you arrive and place your order, much to your chagrin, the sandwich pales in comparison to the one displayed in the advertisement. And, the big drink is watered down because it overflows with ice.

The size and quality of products in nearly every market shrinks while their prices are on a steep incline. Decades ago, these practices would have been considered unthinkable and unacceptable. They now occur because of the greed in our society. That same greed causes men to make decisions benefitting only themselves with no concern or thought as to how their decisions affect anyone else.

Our society's inherent respect for others has been replaced with a distinct disdain for anyone who *considers* the path of respectability. Thinking of others is considered a sign of weakness.

"Kill or be killed" is the motto of this society. People say things like, *"Nothing personal, it's just business."* Statements like this prove that mainstream business is out to hurt and take advantage of those perceived to be weak. This is unacceptable.

Business is the driving force behind any social or economic system. The way in which business is conducted affects every facet of a society.

Enron is a perfect example of how the unscrupulous practices business can and did inflict horror and devastation on an entire society. College funds, pensions, investments, and retirement funds were wiped out in a moment. Why? Simple! Greed caused men to become predators, raping and devouring the perceived weak.

Just like the atomic bombs dropped on Japan in World War II, the affects of Enron's betrayal is still felt today. How many people never went to college because of Enron? How many lost their hope of retiring? How many lost their investments? We may never know.

Enron is not the only culprit, though. The government is just as much to blame as any conniving business executive.

The United States government is irresponsible. When I was a kid, the national deficit was less than 3 trillion dollars. Now, only 25 years later, the national debt has more than quadrupled. This means that when my son approaches thirty, the national debt will have increased close to 7 times.

Also, there is a lack of morality. Every week, it seems as though there is another political leader or elected official caught in some scandal. Cheating on their wives and performing lewd acts in public restrooms are just a few of the immoral acts of this government's leaders.

Business and government have partnered in bringing down the standard of excellence which was once very high. Excellence is no longer a practice, merely a marketing strategy. It hangs high in every store window. It's on every brochure in banks across the globe and makes for good conversation and great entertainment. Sadly, the practice of excellence as well as the practice of respecting others was tossed out right next to the baby and the bath water.

Excellence has been removed from our society and replaced with greed and selfishness. **It must be restored!** If this epidemic had only been confined to the world — Egypt, if you will — it's quite possible we may have been able to tolerate it. But *this* exchange of character has found its ugly way into the Church! The standard of righteousness God established for His house is being lowered every day!

Pastors and Spiritual Leaders shun accountability to live secret lives of sin. Husbands and wives are divorcing at an alarming rate, citing *"irreconcilable differences"* to justify their actions. How can things be *irreconcilable* if we are walking in accordance with scripture?

Teenagers are rebelling from their Christian upbringing to indulge in the pleasures of the world. The lack of couth and character among so-called Christians is heart breaking.

In the Old Testament, a field was defiled if there was more than one type of seed sown in it (Deut 22:9). Only one crop could be planted per field: i.e., corn in one field and wheat in another. You could not, however, plant both corn and wheat in the same field during a given planting season. To do so was to defile the entire field and all its crops.

This may seem strange but it has huge spiritual implications.

In Matthew 13, Jesus spoke about a man sowing good seed in his field. Then, an enemy came in while men slept and sowed tares among the other seed in the same field. To you and me, this may not seem so bad. To those listening to Jesus, though, this was an outrage! They were really taken aback when He finished the parable with the field's owner telling his workers to take the wheat/tares mixture and put it into his barns. According to the Law of Moses, the wheat and the tares should have been destroyed.

In scripture, a field represents our heart. We are only supposed to have one type of seed sown in it – The Word of God! The parable further explains that God is not the only one with seed: the devil also has seed. The key to this parable lies in knowing how the enemy was able to get close enough to plant his seed: he did it while men slept! This means there were men assigned to keep watch over the field to ensure that it stayed pure and the seed uncontaminated.

Proverbs 4:23 instructs us to keep our hearts diligently because all of the issues of our lives are housed there. The men of the parable failed to keep watch over the field. Therefore, the enemy came in and corrupted it.

For the sakes of our families and communities, excellence **must** be restored! We **must** respect people again! We **must not** seek to manipulate others for personal gain! We **must** regain a genuine love and appreciation for serving others! *Then*, we will all prosper *together* and *honor God* in the process.

That is Excellence!

Adrian Taylor, Jr.

Introduction

When building any type of structure, a proper foundation must first be laid. That foundation, however, must be laid in direct proportion to the extravagance of the design of the structure. In other words, the taller the plan for the building, the deeper the foundation must be.

The foundation is the anchor for the building. It holds the entire structure in place. If heavy winds blow, the foundation, like an anchor on the sea floor, securely holds the building in place. It counteracts the environmental forces and provides stability in the most adverse conditions. Thus, the most crucial piece of any structure would be the foundation.

As stated earlier, the foundation is calculated based on the design or vision for the desired structure. As pertaining to our lives, God is the Great Architect. In His design plans, we discover that His desired outcome for each of us is very high. In fact, Jeremiah 29:11 says that His thoughts concerning us are peaceful and not evil: He wants to bring us into a victorious destination. That is a tall order! For such a high design, God has developed a foundation which can easily support us –Jesus!

The foundation for our lives is Jesus Christ!

1 Cor. 3:11 *For other foundation can no man lay than that is laid, which is Jesus Christ.*

Although the foundation is very important, infrastructure is of equal if not more importance. The infrastructure provides shape, form, and character for a building. Most importantly, the infrastructure bears the load and weight of a facility. It prevents the whole thing from falling down and keeps the building firmly attached to the foundation.

An infrastructure can take many forms. The one I have chosen to clearly illustrate this book's focus is the *pillar*.

Pillars are ornate and load-bearing. They offer great imagery and character to any building.

Excellence is the noticeable, external sign of character in a person's life. We *could* say it is the essence of God Himself. Excellence, however, is heavy.

Those who walk in it have great responsibility as well as great blessing. They are honored and hated at the same time. For the sake of our focus, excellence will be the roof – heavy and grandiose. Such a roof requires a solid foundation and a strong, secure infrastructure.

In essence, there are certain spiritual principles we must establish in our lives in order to build and maintain the life God has designed for us. Through the Bible, we will highlight a few of the *Pillars* which need to be constructed so we may walk in excellence. In no way is this book designed to be the sum total of *excellence*. However, it will serve as an awesome tool to guide you in your journey of becoming all God made you to be.

PILLAR ONE
FAITHFULNESS

God Is *Faithful*

> Deuteronomy 7:9   *Know therefore that the Lord thy God, He is God, the <u>faithful</u> God, which keepeth covenant and mercy with them that love him and keeps his commandments to a thousand generations;*

In this passage, *faithful* means trustworthy. It is evident that God is revealing Himself as an individual Who is worthy of our trust.

> 2 Timothy 2:13   *If we believe not, yet he abideth faithful: he cannot deny himself.*

In this verse, God indicates that our inability to trust Him does not prevent Him from being trustful (in this verse, *faithful* means *trustful*) or full of trust. God goes to the extent that He will not deny being faithful to you even when you fail being faithful to Him. We get a divine infusion of faithfulness from the Lord through His gracious willingness to be faithful to us even when we don't deserve it. Praise God!!

Since we are created in God's image and likeness, we should bear His nature. **God is faithful!** In fact, the above verse calls Him the *faithful* God. It is thus implied that God, Who not only possesses a faithful attitude, is the defined essence of *faithful*. Therefore, faithfulness is equal to godliness!

God does not lie. The ability to lie is not in Him. Neither does He play with our emotions or seek to impress us with fancy speech. There are some people who have mastered the fine art of eloquence: they know how to make big promises. They are fluent in their ability to captivate and manipulate. All the while, though, they are merely scheming to get something from us to benefit them… not us.

Every year, politicians tell people what they want to hear in order to gain popularity and votes. Oftentimes, though, something usually presents itself in the future to prevent their following through on their promises. More than likely, their allegiance is to their financial benefactors or political party agenda. Therefore, their words are empty.

On the other hand, the eternal God of Heaven is not bound by political affiliations or any higher powers which prevent Him from fulfilling His word. When **He** speaks something, **He** does it! He *never* says anything He cannot nor intends not to do. He is both willing and able to accomplish *everything* He says. God is committed to every Word He speaks. **Who would not want to be faithful to a God like that?**

God Searches for *Faithful* People

> 1 Samuel 2:35 *And I will raise Me up a faithful priest, that shall do according to that which is in Mine heart and in My mind: and I will build him a sure house; and he shall walk before Mine anointed for ever.*
> Psalm 31:23 *O love the Lord, all ye his saints: for the Lord preserveth the faithful, and plentifully rewardeth the proud doer.*

Psalm 101:6 *Mine eyes shall be upon the faithful of the land, that they may dwell with Me: he that walketh in a perfect way, he shall serve Me.*

Having a faithful heart and life pleases God because it is an honor for Him to see us as direct reflections of Himself. God loves Himself. In other words, He pleases Himself. He made us in His image because He loves to see His pure and holy image everywhere.

When we properly display godly character - faithfulness, commitment, et al – we exhibit the true image of God (that He created us in) and give Him great glory! He does not desire to see us in our sinful and selfish condition which is why He washes us in His Own blood (Rev. 1:5) - to cleanse us from the perversion of carnality.

The more we submit to His will and let go of our selfish ways, the more we shine forth His beauty in the world. If He can't find men who are faithful, God will raise and establish faithful men to bless them greatly.

Characteristics of a *Faithful* Person

1. A Faithful Person lives in accordance with God's Word

Psalm 119:138 *Thy testimonies that Thou hast commanded are righteous and very faithful.*

2. A Faithful Person is Trustworthy

Proverbs 11:13 *A talebearer revealeth secrets: but he that is of a faithful spirit concealeth the matter.*

3.. A Faithful Person is Honest and Truthful

Proverbs 14:5 *A faithful witness will not lie: but a false witness will utter lies.*

4. A Faithful Person is Rare

Proverbs 20:6 *Most men will proclaim every one his own goodness: but a faithful man who can find?*

5. A Faithful Person is Soothing and Refreshing

Proverbs 25:13 *As the cold of snow in the time of harvest, so is a faithful messenger to them that send him: for he refresheth the soul of his masters.*

6. A Faithful Person is Despised and Plotted against

Daniel 6:4 *Then the presidents and princes sought to find occasion against Daniel concerning the kingdom; but they could find none occasion nor fault; forasmuch as he was faithful, neither was there any error or fault found in him.*

7. A Faithful Person Takes Care of the Little Things

Luke 16:10 *He that is faithful in that which is least is faithful also in much: and he that is unjust in the least is unjust also in much.*

The Top Requirement

1 Cor. 4:2 *Moreover it is required in stewards, that a man be found faithful.*

We are all stewards. A steward is someone who is given charge of something not belonging to him. He is entrusted to keep watch over his master's affairs and/or property. At the very least, we are stewards of our bodies and time.

Parents steward their children. Employees are stewards for their bosses. And, we are all stewards for God: to pray, evangelize, study, and serve one another in the Spirit of Love and Joy. Through all of this, God is glorified, men are brought into righteousness, and we gain promotion and increase for our lives.

Yes, we are all stewards for God and it is required of us that we are found to be faithful!

> Luke 18:8b *Nevertheless when the Son of man cometh, shall he find faith on the earth?*

In the context of this verse, the word *faith* is often misunderstood. Faith is more than a spiritual substance of hope. It is possible to be a person who hopes in God and not be a person of faith.

From the Hebraic perspective, faith means to trust in the Lord. In fact, when I asked my big brother Apostle Karockas Watkins about faith, he told me that the Hebrew people view faith as, "trusting; to lean on God as a man would lean on a wall."

When a person leans on a solid wall, he never considers that the wall will fail him. He rests confidently on that wall without fear. He never doubts because he knows that whether the ground shakes some or the wind blows, even if he slips, the wall will keep him standing. That is a perfect understanding of how we are to trust in or have faith in God.

In Luke 18, the Lord says He will come again. And when He does, He asks a question: Will He find faith on the earth? However, what He is really asking is, will He find a *faithful* people.

Have you ever noticed that, even among Christian people, there are so many who claim to have *faith* in God but are untrustworthy and unreliable? They make commitments to do things but don't follow through. Almost any problem or disruption prevents their being faithful. They are full of excuses and blame others. This is a contradiction of faithfulness. People of faith *must* be *faithful*!

We talked about God being the *Faithful* God: this is extremely important. The only reason we can lean so confidently on the Lord without fear is not because *we* are so faithful. Rather, it is because *He* is so faithful.

Abraham believed God and was called righteous because He *trusted* God (Romans 4:3). In other words, Abraham determined that God is so faithful, he *could* trust Him. Abraham put His whole life and family in God's capable hands because he learned that God would never fail Him.

God is *faithful*! His name is ***faithful***! Now, He is searching for a *faithful* people, a people who have become so convinced that the Lord is true to His Word, they can rely on Him. Those are the people who will follow the steps outlined in this chapter for becoming faithful.

PILLAR ONE FINAL NOTE

A Country preacher once told me something very significant. Having been a pastor for 25 years, he said this:

"In all my years, I have not been perfect. I haven't done everything right. But one thing I have been: I have been faithful. All God is looking for you to be is faithful."

I think about that statement a lot. Punctuality and faithfulness are not the same. A person can have a great reputation for being punctual. But, if he is frequently absent, his faithfulness is lacking. Think of it this way: I know some people who are always late for most things. But, these same people can be depended upon to complete any assignment they are given. They may not be the ideal candidate in most people's books. But for me, faithfulness is far more important than punctuality.

Please hear my message: I am in no way promoting tardiness. The person who is tardy may not win a popularity contest but he can earn the perfect attendance award.

Strive not to be perfect or to be right all the time. Rather, develop a life of faithfulness.

Your Jericho March To Excellence

1. What does faithfulness mean to you?

2. How has God shown His faithfulness to you?

3. When has your faithfulness to God and excellence been tested?

4. What can you do to raise your level of faithfulness?

5. Practice faithfulness for the next 7 days. Journal about your experience here.

PILLAR 2

Discipline

Disciple is the root word of *discipline*. If anyone is going to become disciplined in anything, he must first submit to a trainer or a coach.

The original 12 Apostles were first called *disciples*. They had to surrender to a strict code of ethics and a rigorous routine. Jesus accepted no excuses. If you were not willing to pay the price of discipleship, he would not waste His time mentoring you.

Disciple:

1. Religion.

   a. one of the 12 personal followers of Christ, or any follower of Christ.

2. A person who is a pupil or an adherent of the doctrines of another; follower.

Discipline:

1. Training expected to produce a specific character or pattern of behavior, especially training that produces moral or mental improvement.

2. Controlled behavior resulting from disciplinary training; self-control.

   a. Control obtained by enforcing compliance or order.
   b. A systematic method to obtain obedience: *a military discipline.*
   c. A state of order based on submission to rules and authority

The Cost of Discipleship

Luke 14:25-33 *And there went great multitudes with Him: and He turned, and said unto them, [26] If any man come to Me, and hate not his father, and mother, and wife, and children, and brethren, and sisters, yea, and his own life also, he cannot be My disciple. [27] And whosoever doth not bear his cross, and come after Me, cannot be My disciple. [28] For which of you, intending to build a tower, sitteth not down first, and counteth the cost, whether he have sufficient to finish it? [29] Lest haply, after he hath laid the foundation, and is not able to finish it, all that behold it begin to mock him, [30] Saying, This man began to build, and was not able to finish.*

[31] Or what king, going to make war against another king, sitteth not down first, and consulteth whether he be able with ten thousand to meet him that cometh against him with twenty thousand? [32] Or else, while the other is yet a great way off, he sendeth an ambassage, and desireth conditions of peace. [33] So likewise, whosoever he be of you that forsaketh not all that he hath, he cannot be My disciple.

Jesus' sole purpose for saying this was to point out the severity of being His disciple. He takes the business of discipleship extremely seriously: He wants a person to be unequivocally certain that following Him is what they desire.

He mentions the preparatory responsibility of calculating the total expense before you start working. In other words, you need to know what is involved in being His disciple.

A restaurant menu lists the entrées in large, **bold** letters. But, the side dishes and descriptions are written in fine print underneath: you have to read the small print to know what you are going to eat. So also must you read what is expected, in fact, what is demanded, by Jesus of all His followers.

Here is the list Jesus outlined in the above verses:

1. You must hate your family and your own life also.

2. You must bare your cross and follow Him.

3. You must forsake all that you have.

Firstly, no person can be more important than the Lord – not even you.

Secondly, you must be willing to follow Jesus wherever he goes, even to death. You must be willing to lay your life down as He laid down His. Jesus carried His cross to His death: you must carry your cross to your death also. Remember that, as you die, He rises within you with newness of life.

Thirdly, you must not hold any possession or thing more important than him. Nothing you have belongs to you. Anything you possess is at His disposal. If He requests anything from you, you must give it freely.

As a Disciple of Christ, you must submit to the Lord and diligently adhere to His teaching and wisdom. If you cannot obey *Another*, then, you will not have the strength to bring discipline to yourself. A good coach challenges a player to grow and develop in the skills he needs to succeed. We have to see Jesus as our coach. The power to conquer one's own urges and flesh is unleashed when you are in humble and faithful submission to Christ.

A Proper Balance of Spirit & Truth

John 4:24 *God is a Spirit: and they that worship Him must worship Him in spirit and in truth.*
John 17:17 *Sanctify them through Thy truth: Thy word is truth.*
1 John 5:6 *This is He that came by water and blood, even Jesus Christ; not by water only, but by water and blood. And it is the Spirit that beareth witness, because the Spirit is truth.*

The power to be spiritually disciplined requires a delicate balance of Spirit and Truth. What does that mean? The Holy Spirit and the Word of God work together. The Holy Spirit and the Word of God also agree in every way possible. You have to submit to the teaching of the Lord, His Word. Then, you must obey *Them*. In order to do that, you must be filled with and led by the Holy Spirit.

It is impossible for anybody in this world to follow the instructions of the Lord without the Holy Spirit dwelling in him. It is equally impossible for the Holy Spirit to work mightily in our lives without the Word of God being in us.

Philippians 2:13 *For it is God which worketh in you both to will and to do of His good pleasure.*

There must be a proper balance in us: one of receiving the Word and obeying the Word by the Spirit of God. He gave us His Word **and** He gave us His Spirit so we could be faithful to Him without excuse.

As the Word of God dominates our hearts, transformation

takes place inside. In essence, our internal desires change: God's desire becomes our desire as we hear, study, and meditate on the Word of God. The Word provides guidelines ensuring that we are moving in alignment with the Spirit.

Since the Spirit and the Word are One, we can rest assured that, because we are faithful in the Word, we are truly being Spirit-led. As a result, the Holy Spirit provides tools to help us overcome our sinful nature. He uses the Word inside of us as a sword to cut down demonic influence and carnal desire. Therefore, we are changed from the inside out as we grow in the Word and yield to the Spirit. This is proper spiritual balance.

There are some who love to claim *spiritual* maturity. Unfortunately, the things they do often have no biblical foundation or support. Dreams and visions are nice. Yet, without understanding from the Bible, we will soon be very much misled. The Bible is our handy guidebook for all things spiritual.

Then, there are those who are so dogmatic and legalistic in their Bible focus, they attempt to live the Bible existentially.

Now, I don't care what type car you own. Although it may be immaculate, without the proper fuel, it is going nowhere!! These folks who try to live existentially are misled in believing that spiritual things are not pure. However, without the indwelling of the Holy Spirit and His internal influence, we all are powerless to perform the things God outlines for us in scripture.

Temperance

1 Cor. 9:25-27 *And every man that striveth for the mastery is temperate in all things. Now they do it to obtain a corruptible crown; but we an incorruptible. [26] I therefore so run, not as uncertainly; so fight I, not as one that beateth the air: [27] But I keep under my body, and bring it into subjection: lest that by any means, when I have preached to others, I myself should be a castaway.*

Temperance, one of the most unappreciated gifts of the Holy Spirit, is simply self control. This is the gift which instills in us the power to control ourselves. Some people say they could not help themselves. They can't help themselves because they did not surrender to the Holy Spirit and allow Him to work temperance in their lives.

Why do men sin? No temperance. Why are men willing to risk everything they have for a one-night stand? No self-control. Because they were not walking in the power of temperance, they gave in to pressure and temptation overpowered them! Their *self* was out of control like a car without an alert driver.

Temperance vs. Temptation

Continence: self-restraint or abstinence, esp. in regard to sexual activity; temperance; moderation.

> 1 Cor. 9:25 *And every man that striveth for the mastery is temperate in all things. Now they do it to obtain a corruptible crown; but we an incorruptible.*
> James 1:12 *Blessed is the man that endureth temptation: for when he is tried, he shall receive the crown of life, which the Lord hath promised to them that love him.*

Temperance is a spiritual gift provided by the Holy Spirit. Its primary evidence is self-control and continence. Temperance is like the wall of a strong city; no matter what pressure or siege there may be in our life, temperance stands firm without wavering. It is sheer focus in the face of great difficulty.

Temptation doesn't stand a chance against temperance! In fact, a person doesn't actually know if he is temperate *until* temptation arises. Temptation flows like water searching to penetrate the weakest and most vulnerable spots of a person's life. It desires to pull you out of the strength of the Spirit so it may contaminate and destroy you.

Temperance, on the other hand, establishes an impenetrable, water-proof barrier. If you stand firm in temperance, no temptation can gain a foothold or access point into your soul. God, then, rewards the one who endures temptation with a crown of life (James 1:12). If God honors those who endure temptation, then, it behooves us, as His children, to get in on this endowment by holding fast to *Temperance*.

The Threat of Temptation

Temptation:
1. Something that seduces or has the quality to seduce.
2. The desire to have or do something you know you should avoid: "*he felt the temptation and his will-power weakened*".
3. The act of influencing by exciting hope or desire: "*his enticements were shameless*".
4. The act of tempting: enticement or allurement.

1 Cor. 10:13   *There hath no temptation taken you but such as is common to man: but God is faithful, who will not suffer you to be tempted above that ye are able; but will with the temptation also make a way to escape, that ye may be able to bear it.*

No one is exempt from temptation! Everyone will be enticed and will, at times, succumb to the pressure of its seductive allure.

I Corinthians 10:13 states that there is actually a *common* temptation. Most people try to isolate their situation as if it is somehow unique: they have a *special burden* no one understands. This is foolish and designed to do only one thing: divide a person from others so he can be destroyed without anyone knowing his situation or coming to his aide. The beautiful thing, though, is that, no matter how long or difficult a situation may be, God has given us a hope, a way of escape!

Matthew 26:41   *Watch and pray, that ye enter not into temptation: the spirit indeed is willing, but the flesh is weak.*
Mark 14:38 *Watch ye and pray, lest ye enter into temptation. The spirit truly is ready, but the flesh is weak.*

Temptation strikes at the weakest part of our being: the flesh! Jesus told us that the flesh is weak. Another verse states that there is no profit in the flesh (Luke 6:63). The spirit displays a constant, alacritous, cheerful readiness at all times. It continually bares a focused disposition.

Therefore, temptation labors very hard to pull a person out of the spirit and into the flesh. The flesh is weak and unprofitable.

Anyone who walks in the flesh will be weak and unprofitable as well.

The Discipline to Endure Temptation

Mark 14:38 *Watch ye and pray, lest ye enter into temptation. The spirit truly is ready, but the flesh is weak.*

The Lord instructs us to watch and pray or we will enter into temptation. Watching and praying does not prevent temptation, it merely positions us to stand against its attack. Watching and praying keeps us in the Spirit: the place where temperance optimally functions. So, watch and pray to stay strong and profitable.

Endurance Determines Discipline

Endurance:
How long something lasts...
How strong something is...
How durable something is...
How much integrity something possesses...
How much pressure something can handle...
The life expectancy of a thing...

Psalm 102:12 *But Thou, O Lord, shalt endure for ever; and Thy remembrance unto all generations.*
Matthew 24:13 *But he that shall endure unto the end, the same shall be saved.*
Mark 4:17 *And have no root in themselves, and so endure but for a time: afterward, when affliction or persecution ariseth for the word's sake, immediately they are offended.*
Mark 13:13 *And ye shall be hated of all men for My name's sake: but he that shall endure unto the end, the same shall be saved.*
2 Thess. 1:4 *So that we ourselves glory in you in the churches of God for your patience and faith in all your persecutions and tribulations that ye endure:*

2 Tim. 2:3 *Thou therefore endure hardness, as a good soldier of Jesus Christ.*
2 Tim. 2:10 *Therefore I endure all things for the elect's sakes, that they may also obtain the salvation which is in Christ Jesus with eternal glory.*
2 Tim. 4:3 *For the time will come when they will not endure sound doctrine; but after their own lusts shall they heap to themselves teachers, having itching ears;*
2 Tim. 4:5 *But watch thou in all things, endure afflictions, do the work of an evangelist, make full proof of thy ministry.*
Hebrews 12:7 *If ye endure chastening, God dealeth with you as with sons; for what son is he whom the father chasteneth not?*

A disciplined person follows instructions and implements his training… **regardless** of his environment. The system of influence operating inside of him is far greater than the influences outside of him. Temperance provides him with a secure environment to execute his training and *prove* his discipline.

PILLAR TWO FINAL NOTE

During my sophomore year in high school, I enrolled in Jr. R.O.T.C. and joined the Drill Team. My classmates had already joined the Drill Team the previous year. So, they were far more advanced than I. However, I practiced and trained extremely hard.

It was insane! During the middle of the cold, St. Louis winter (below freezing), you found me outside: no gloves, spinning my rifle, throwing it in the air, hurting my hand catching it, over and over, marching up and down the streets and alleys. Needless to say, I wanted to catch up with my classmates.

At the end of that year, we were invited to an all-city Drill Competition hosted by the Army Reserves. It was a big-time event! R.O.T.C. programs from all over the City of St. Louis and surrounding areas were there. Our school had not competed in years and we were very nervous (at least I was).

Actual military personnel judged the competition, judging each group on uniform, execution, difficulty, and discipline. For example: for discipline, if you messed up or something went bad (and it did), they wanted to know how you were going to respond. An intimidating presence, those Drill Sergeants walked around every team as they performed. They watched even the tiniest expressions on each person's face.

Well, our turn to compete came. We were performing with rifles. There was a maneuver we performed called an *"exchange."* In this maneuver, two or more people simultaneously throw their rifles to each other. A simple enough maneuver, most teams do some variation of an exchange; but we were doing a precision four-corner exchange.

Basically, we were in a box formation with four people facing diagonally inward. Each person was to throw his rifle to the person directly across from him. In other words, four rifles were going to cross each other in mid-air at the same time (a slight, second delay would cause their collision).

Needless to say, this move had to be timed exactly right. One second too early, and all four rifles would come crashing to the floor in front of all the best Drill Teams in St. Louis. A few moments too late, and we risked throwing off the remainder of the entire performance. We were under a lot of pressure and the moment of truth came.

We faced inward towards our exchange partners. I faced my partner, placed my rifle on the floor, kicked it backward for momentum, and tossed it straight across to him just as we had practiced hundreds of times before. I was *so* glad I did it correctly! But, in that same moment when it should have, his rifle **did not** come straight to me!

This is one of those slow-motion moments you see in the movies. My mind was going crazy as I watched his rifle flying to my far left: his angle was somehow off. It was now up to me to save this performance.

I was so terribly nervous but remembered my training. I looked at all the judges and my teammates. Composing myself, I lunged to my left, stretched as far as my arms would allow, and caught the flailing rifle, just narrowly saving my teammate to my left from a trip to the hospital. Somehow, I was able to capture the rifle and place us back in flow to complete the performance.

We placed 3rd for that performance. Had I allowed that undesirable moment to affect me, if I had forsaken my discipline, we would not have placed in that event. I was credited by my whole team as the guy who saved the performance. I remained disciplined in the face of great opposition.

Your Jericho March To Excellence

1. **What does discipline mean to you?**

2. **How have you developed discipline in your Christian walk?**

3. **Has your level of discipline declined? If so, in what way?**

4. **What can you do to raise your level of discipline?**

5. **Practice discipline for the next 7 days. Journal about your experience here.**

PILLAR 3
Obedience

Obey is the root word of *obedience*. To obey is to follow instructions. The principle of obedience is an essential link to mastering maturity in the Christian lifestyle. As you will see, obedience determines and proves the type of character a person has.

The Nature of Obedience

Obedience:
- Attentive Hearkening
- Compliant Submission

> Deut. 11:26-28 *Behold, I set before you this day a blessing and a curse; [27] A blessing, if ye obey the commandments of the Lord your God, which I command you this day:*
> *[28] And a curse, if ye will not obey the commandments of the Lord your God, but turn aside out of the way which I command you this day, to go after other gods, which ye have not known.*

There are two items of note in this passage:
(1) Obedience produces a blessed and prosperous life.
(2) Disobedience produces a cursed and villainous life.

> Romans 6:16 *Know ye not, that to whom ye yield yourselves servants to obey, his servants ye are to whom ye obey; whether of sin unto death, or of obedience unto righteousness?*

In the above verse, a person is the servant to whom he or she obeys. Because his master is greater than he is, a servant serves his master. Whomever you obey is who you are bound to as a servant: your services to them make them greater than you.

From the one you obey, you will receive a reward. If you obey God then, your service to Him warrants eternal life, blessing, and prosperous favor for you. If you obey sin then, you will receive loss, death, and destruction from sin!

The Cost of Obedience

> 1 Samuel 15:22 *And Samuel said, Hath the Lord as great delight in burnt offerings and sacrifices, as in obeying the voice of the Lord? Behold, to obey is better than sacrifice, and to hearken than the fat of rams.*

We must understand that obedience is **not** an option. We are told to obey the Lord without compromise. This is costly. Which means, how much more do you value God than whatever He asks of you?

Most people are only willing to give God what **they** want to give Him. But, what if He asks for more than you want to give? Will you obey? Do you realize that the sacrifice you will have to make in order to please God is nothing compared to the blessing and honor promised to you if you would just do what he requests?

God Always Watches Your Heart

> Isaiah 1:19 *If ye be willing and obedient, ye shall eat the good of the land:*
> 1 Samuel 16:7 *But the Lord said unto Samuel, Look not on his countenance, or on the height of his stature; because I have refused him: for the Lord seeth not as man seeth; for man looketh on the outward appearance, but the Lord looketh on the heart.*
> Exodus 25:2-3 *Speak unto the children of Israel, that they bring Me an offering: of every man that giveth it willingly with his heart ye shall take My offering. [3] And this is the offering which ye shall take of them; gold, and silver, and brass,*

A person must be *willing* to obey. Remember: the heart with which you do something is what God is interested in. He will tell us to do something and then watch our attitude while we're doing it. Even though you may have obeyed, God may not receive it if it was not offered properly. The proper way to offer anything to God is always with a *willing* heart.

Obedience Proves Your Love for God

> 1 John 5:2-3 *By this we know that we love the children of God, when we love God, and keep his commandments. [3] For this is the love of God, that we keep his commandments: and*

his commandments are not grievous.

Luke 6:46-49 *And why call ye Me, Lord, Lord, and do not the things which I say? [47] Whosoever cometh to Me, and heareth My sayings, and doeth them, I will shew you to whom he is like:[48] He is like a man which built an house, and digged deep, and laid the foundation on a rock: and when the flood arose, the stream beat vehemently upon that house, and could not shake it: for it was founded upon a rock. [49] But he that heareth, and doeth not, is like a man that without a foundation built an house upon the earth; against which the stream did beat vehemently, and immediately it fell; and the ruin of that house was great.*

Our love for God is also our motivating factor for obeying Him. If we truly love God, we will **promptly** obey Him.

The scripture says, *"His commandments are not grievous."* They are not too hard to accomplish. In fact, our love for God produces a *willingness* to serve Him. Our heart's desire is to serve the Lord with *willing* obedience. Through love, obeying God is not a chore. Rather, it is a pure delight.

PILLAR THREE FINAL NOTE

When I was a kid, we used to sing a song in children's church that went like this:

"Obedience is the very best way to show that you believe.
O-B-E-D-I-E-N-C-E
Obedience is the very best way to show that you believe."

That song has resonated with me now for decades. (Thank you, Sister Rita!) I love it for so many reasons. First, it was simple. Second, it taught us how to spell a truly important spiritual word. Lastly, it spoke a clear truth that will last throughout eternity- ***Obedience is the very best way to show that you believe.*** I love it!!

Think of it this way; I can do various things for my wife or son to demonstrate my love for either of them. However, we can only offer one thing to God that will verify that our confessions of undying love for Him are much more than just empty words... **obedience**.

If you love the Lord, then, **obey Him**!

Your Jericho March To Excellence

1. **What does obedience mean to you?**

2. **How have you developed obedience in your Christian walk?**

3. **When and how has your obedience to God been tested?**

4. **What can you do to raise your level of obedience?**

5. **Practice obedience for the next 7 days. Journal about your experience here.**

PILLAR 4

The Law of Preparation

The *Law of Preparation* is a spiritual principle which keeps a person in a constant state of readiness. Being in a state of readiness allows an individual to stay focused and not be caught off guard. Many people live in a contrary *State of Procrastination*.

Apostle Halton "*Skip*" Horton defines procrastination as "disobedience in slow motion." A vast majority of people, especially Christians, are constantly late and behind schedule. Because of this, there is an increased level of anxiety, stress, and undue frustration all caused by the pressure of a rushed lifestyle.

****

The typical day of *Norman Rushsomemore* normally begins with the alarm clock buzzing, his disheveled head lifting from the pillow, frantically flinging his hand toward the alarm. After a series of misguided swings, his hand manages to batter the irate '*snooze*' button into submission, silencing the noise.

Again, like a banshee, the alarm shrieks and Norman repeats his earlier brutal attack. This goes on for what seems like only minutes when Mr. Rushsomemore catches a glimpse of his clock. He realizes he has slept ages too long. Instantly, he jumps up! Sheets flying, Norman jolts out of bed scampering to the bathroom.

In the bathroom, amid hot steam from the shower and toothpaste drizzling from his open mouth, Norman strains to hear the morning weather and traffic reports bellowing from the next room. Now, attempts to calculate the quickest route for his morning drive join with the inundating thoughts of his continued tardiness flood his already cluttered mind.

He speeds through a shower and grabs some clothes to iron. After dressing and a few final primps, he runs through the house grabbing his papers and thrusting them into his shoulder bag. He tosses food to the dog, opens shutters for the sunlight to hit the plants, and shoves one arm into his coat while scurrying out the door.

You already know how this story concludes: Norman gets stuck in traffic. Agitated by yet another disappointing delay, he rages his way through traffic only to catch the eager eye of the police. By the time he arrives at work, he is angry, flustered, and extremely late. However, he *does* have a traffic ticket to offer as an excuse to his boss.

Not surprisingly, Norman is already behind in his work. He arrives late most days and never completes anything on time. Each day, work from the previous days spill over into the next causing him to remain at work much later and never catching up or moving ahead.

Unfortunately, his life is so chaotic that his only reward at the end of the day is the comfort of an unmade bed in the midst of a house which appears to have scarcely survived a bout with a tornado.

Sad to say, most people are in a state similar to Norman Rushsomemore. What was his profound issue? Easy! He was not prepared! Thus, he is stuck in a constant cycle of *getting ready* and *catching up*.

****

When we are not prepared, we are already behind schedule because we did not move with prudence. The proper use of time is a necessary skill, one which all mankind must master in order to be effective.

Most people are constantly *getting* ready. But *getting* ready when you should be moving forward instantly pushes you back in time into a state of *catching up*. The more time you waste getting ready, the longer it takes to catch up. So many people never catch up because they have grown too weary.

Preparation

1. The act or process of preparing.
2. The state of having been made ready beforehand; readiness.
3. A preliminary measure that serves to make ready for something. Often used in the plural: *preparations for the wedding.*

The second definition speaks of being *made ready beforehand.* This is the heart of what it means to be prepared. Instead of just wasting time and laying around, a person has to utilize foresight in order to be in a constant state of readiness.

For example, ironing clothes the night before is a wise use of time. It prepositions a person for their day by making them more able to function the next day. The time which was previously used to get ready in the morning can now be used to meditate or pray. It also allows a person to move more smoothly because his mind is focused. He is now in a position to be proactive instead of reactive. He determines the flow of his day instead of the day determining his flow.

Prudence

Proverbs 22:3 *A prudent man foreseeth the evil, and hideth himself: but the simple pass on, and are punished.*

One key element of the Law of Preparation is *prudence*. Prudence is the ability to foresee: to look ahead and make adjustments now which avoid future destruction.

At the same time, prudent foresight allows a person to take advantage of opportunities he would not normally be ready for... because he was so busy trying to catch up, he couldn't even recognize that an opportunity was at hand. In other words, we often miss out on good benefits and opportunities because we are preoccupied dealing with things we should have already done.

For example; the morning news provides traffic reports on accidents and weather to assist people in their daily travel planning. In fact, these reports often suggest better travel routes if more popular passageways are blocked. The prudent man will make time to watch the morning travel report because it offers valuable insights for his day. If the need arises, he can make changes in his morning drive.

On the other hand, if a person neglects watching the morning news because he woke up late and runs through the house trying to get ready, he causes greater delays to occur. He misses an important opportunity to get back on track because of preventable distractions.

The Day of Preparation

Keeping the Sabbath day was and still is a common practice among Jewish people. Typically, the Sabbath begins at 6:00 p.m. (sundown) every Friday evening and ends at the same time on Saturday evening. The Sabbath is a holy day designed for rest and honoring the Lord.

On the Sabbath, no work is allowed. Traditional Jewish customs only allow for a restricted amount of walking and activity.

This day is a highly regimented day. Therefore, the Jewish people operate in the Law of Preparation. In fact, the day before the Sabbath is called, *"The Preparation."*

This day is utilized as a time to make all the necessary preparations to be ready for the Sabbath. Whatever business needs to be carried out or whatever provisions are needed for life to continue while they keep the Sabbath is made during *The Preparation.* It is a day for making ready: a time of *prudence.*

David's Preparation

> 1 Chronicles 22:5 *And David said, Solomon my son is young and tender, and the house that is to be builded for the Lord must be exceeding magnifical, of fame and of glory throughout all countries: I will therefore now make preparation for it. So David prepared abundantly before his death.*

David had always wanted to build a house for God: a temple. However, because of the blood on David's hands, God would not allow it. Although David could not build God's house, he still took advantage of his time. He knew God wanted the temple built. Using prudent foresight, he prepared the provisions for the temple.

Once Solomon was chosen to be the next King, David called his son into his chamber and handed him the key to the royal warehouse. He told his son to build God's house. Since he was forbidden to build the temple himself, David made provision throughout his life, laying aside everything needed for his son to carry out his greatest desire.

David made preparation for his son. All Solomon had to do was walk down to the royal warehouse and he would find everything he needed! David had stored up gold, silver, and precious stones. If Solomon needed bricks, they were in the warehouse. If he needed scarlet or purple linens, David had it stored already.

Because David was a man of preparation, all Solomon had to

do was build according to the plan God wanted without need for concern. Solomon could save time: he did not need to waste time raising funds or collecting materials because his father had already done it. The temple carries Solomon's name because of his father. David had the *prudence* to use his time wisely so Solomon could use his time effectively.

The Ant

> Proverbs 6:6-11 *Go to the ant, thou sluggard; consider her ways, and be wise: [7] Which having no guide, overseer, or ruler, [8] Provideth her meat in the summer, and gathereth her food in the harvest. [9] How long wilt thou sleep, O sluggard? when wilt thou arise out of thy sleep? [10] Yet a little sleep, a little slumber, a little folding of the hands to sleep: [11] So shall thy poverty come as one that travelleth, and thy want as an armed man.*

Even the ant operates in the *Law of Preparation*! The above scripture clearly points out that the ant uses one season (summer) to provide for the future. The ant diligently uses his time to lay aside provision for the coming winter. Most of us consider ants to be a nuisance. Upon closer investigation, however, we find that they are our teachers. They instruct us on how to be diligent.

Ants search out and find food. They communicate with their colleagues and work together to store up an abundant supply for their entire colony for an entire year. Their most astounding characteristic is that no one has to tell them what to do. Nobody has to supervise or watch over them. No one has to pump them up or coerce them to do their job: they do this of their own accord. Ants are not lazy and do not offer excuses. They operate in *prudence*.

You can eliminate instability by being prepared. It is possible to be prepared for anything by being *prudent*. Once you use foresight to determine the potential obstacles and opportunities you will face, you can make adjustments to avoid danger and be ready to benefit from any situation.

Now, you may not be able to pin-point every issue that may simply *pop up* to catch you off guard. But, you can wisely handle them if your day is not overwhelmed with the distractions of catching up. Being prepared keeps you ahead of the game and enables you to have certain buffers in place which keep you stress-free and focused.

Think right now about what you can do to be prepared for tomorrow. Sacrifice some television time to make ready for future meetings and obligations. Think ahead! Stop **getting ready** and *be prepared*!

Most people claiming to be getting ready are actually behind schedule. Prepare your clothes ahead of time. Prepare your car the night before by putting gas in it. Have your presentations and notes organized in your travel bag beforehand. In doing this, your mind will be at ease: you can think more clearly and be more productive.

Remove the Clutter

Take time to organize yourself. Remove clutter from your life so you can move more freely. The time you waste *looking* for things can be redeemed if you just *get organized*. Clean your closet. Have a hamper for your dirty clothes. Stop throwing everything on your desk and bookshelf. **Throw away junk!**

Clutter breeds chaos. Chaos leads to anarchy. Anarchy's real name is confusion and God is not the originator of confusion (1 Corinthians 14:33). Begin your preparation by cleaning up and removing clutter. Install more *Prep* time in order to **save** time.

Stop being a lazy sluggard who offers excuses! If you rely on the crutch of excuses, you will never stop limping. The Law of Preparation enables you to enjoy a better future by structuring a smoother flow to your daily life.

PILLAR FOUR FINAL NOTE

I recently learned in my Biblical Counseling Course that a crisis is a temporary situation which alters a person's life from his regular routine. That crisis could be an external situation or an internal malfunction. However, regardless of the cause, it is not supposed to be permanent, it should be resolved in six weeks or less.

The problem, though, is that many people - me included - have adopted a crisis mentality. Crisis mode has become our way of life. This occurs because of a lack of proper preparation. Therefore, people are always playing catch up… and, they can never *quite* get ahead.

Normal things like renewing your Driver's License or paying your car Registration become difficult, monumental tasks. These events, normal dynamics of life, should be easily handled. Yet, for those of us who are unprepared, they throw our lives into chaos. A simple deviation in one day's routine, such as going to the DMV to make a payment, turns into a crisis extending far beyond the allotted six-week expiration date for a crisis.

I found this one point to be most interesting, though: a crisis is *only* a crisis if it affects me internally. Panic, anxiety, and fear are often the driving factors of a crisis. They transform normal, unexpected situations into troublesome problems. If you are internally strong with a confident disposition that knows that God is guiding you through, this seeming crisis will soon fade and be peacefully settled.

In other words, our goal is to grow so confident in God's faithfulness to us, we are not moved by even the most intimidating circumstances. Not because **we** are so great, but, because of the greatness of the God that saved us and lives inside of us. He is stronger and wiser than any opposition. Therefore, there *is* no crisis because, by His Spirit, God has deposited within us the peace to calm any storm.

So, let us diligently implement the principles of *The Law of Preparation* in our lives. In doing so, we can easily conquer crisis and demonstrate the superiority of a life filled with faith in God.

Your Jericho March To Excellence

1. Do you follow the Law of Preparation or have you settled in a State of Procrastination? Explain your situation.

2. How have you developed prudence in your Christian walk?

3. When and how has your preparation for the things of God been tested?

4. What can you do to raise your level of preparedness?

5. Follow the path of the ant for the next 7 days. Journal about your experience here.

PILLAR 5
Counting The Cost

Luke 14:28-30 *For which of you, intending to build a tower, sitteth not down first, and counteth the cost, whether he have sufficient to finish it? [29] Lest haply, after he hath laid the foundation, and is not able to finish it, all that behold it begin to mock him, [30] Saying, This man began to build, and was not able to finish.*

For every intention, whether personal or business-related, an in-depth, strategic plan must be meticulously calculated. The purpose of such a plan is two-fold:

1. To ascertain whether an idea can be accomplished.
2. To determine what measures need to be implemented in order to successfully move forward.

Jesus makes this concept plain in the above verse. No actions can be taken if there are not enough resources in place. To do so is to become a '*laughingstock*.' That's right: the Lord said that men would mock you!

All things in life require proper planning. A business demands a business plan. A household functions well with a budget. The plan allows you to know what you can afford. Many people rush into things without realizing the costs involved. Some start businesses or go into ministry without counting the total cost.

Cost is not merely monetary, there are also time considerations. What emotional implications will you experience? What toll will your efforts take on your family? These and many other thoughts must be clearly ascertained and considered before one begins working.

Because most people never count the true cost of being married, the divorce rate is extremely high. Most are either just captivated with a person or just want to have sex. These are two terrible reasons to get married! I can promise you, without counting the cost and making preparations for marriage, your fascination and desire to have sex with your spouse will soon flee your home. Very little effort is placed on marital preparation or establishing a vision for a life together.

Sure, there are many meager marriage counseling classes offered by various churches. And for all of that, the divorce rate *continues* to skyrocket!

I hate to tell you but, if we don't spend more time **organizing** our marriages *prior* to the wedding day than we do planning the wedding, the marriage will last about as long as the reception.

Vision

Proverbs 29:18a *Where there is no vision, the people perish:*

This verse is quite clear: people die without vision! A vision establishes purpose, direction, and, ultimately, destination. Having that type of information helps a person consider wisely the costs necessary for anything.

For instance, if someone were to travel from Seattle to Miami by car, he would need to know:

- The distance between the two cities;
- Which highways are best suited for the journey;
- What potential hazards there are between Seattle and Miami;
- and, how much food and fuel will cost.

A vision is the prudent plan one develops long **before** they get started.

Now, when dealing with God, one must understand that He will not always make every dynamic of His plan clear to us at the onset. However, God will most certainly provide you with a good idea.

Like a good General Contractor, the Lord will offer a good upfront estimate of cost to you. Why is it not exact? Well, oftentimes, we include our own efforts and desires into God's plan. Unfortunately, we can all attest that this is quite disruptive, destructive, and costly! If we don't cooperate with the Holy Spirit (by sticking to the vision He reveals to us), then, we add to the overall cost.

Step Back

Please allow me to take a step back. Although I am writing on the assumption that the reader is spiritual-minded, I realize that true vision is provided to us through divine revelation after much prayer and study of God's Word.

Years ago, I was told by my 10th grade geometry teacher, Ms. Thomas, *"Don't assume anything!"* Most of you know the rest so I will not complete the phrase (as I pause to chuckle.)

True vision comes out of a personal relationship with God. This book is about the *pillars* or *principles* of a life of **excellence**.

Therefore, it is at least implicit in this writing that spiritual maturity must, at minimum, be our objective if not already our current way of life. Even still, no matter how mature we are, we can stand a lot more humility so we can grow into the fullness of Christ.

What does this mean for us? A life of consistent prayer and faith built on strong exegetical study of the Bible will help us focus enough to receive the true vision God has for us, not the man-made ideas people have for us or even our own plan.

Only the plans of God succeed! When we seek to disregard the Eternal Wisdom of God, or worse, mingle our own selfish ambitions with God's plans, we distort things, become confused, waste time, and cause things to be more costly. Remember, we are still talking about 'counting the cost.'

Because the things we do for God are often unseen, faith is very important to this process. Though unseen, these things are far more real than the natural world into which we were born.

Faith, as I shared in Chapter 1, is trusting in God's faithfulness. Since we know God is more committed to bringing His vision into reality than we are, we never have to be afraid. Even when we don't see certain resources or money in place, we are more confident in God's treasury than our own bank account.

When counting the cost, money and natural resources are good. But, faith is far better because it pleases God and He rewards it (Hebrews 11:6). Although God wants us to have natural provision, He does not want us to be *confident* in it. When money runs out, faith still provides. Faith opens doors and allows favor to flow.

Having strong faith through a sound knowledge of the scriptures allows you to do far more than what can be accomplished by natural ability or provision.

This is how Nehemiah functioned. He never lost sight of His vision to rebuild the wall. He prayed for God's direction and favor. Through faith in God, Nehemiah had favor which brought forth provision.

The provision came in the form of assistance from the influential. This same provision also motivated the people to work and kept his enemies at bay. At the end of 52 days, Nehemiah was able to accomplish more than was humanly possible **because** he trusted in God.

Therefore, when making plans and focusing on your vision, don't ask if you have enough money to **accomplish** a task: rather, ask yourself if you have enough *faith*! I digress.

What *Should* I Be Counting?

> Matthew 24:13 *But he that shall endure unto the end, the same shall be saved.*
> 2 Tim. 2:3 *Thou therefore endure hardness, as a good soldier of Jesus Christ.*

I could provide you with a list of *things* to consider. Certainly, there is much to consider when making plans and seeking to progress. (*I believe other sections of this book address them thoroughly.*) Still, a person of excellence is far more than a structured or organized individual. There has to be an undying commitment to completion. You must be committed to the plan God has for you.

When counting the cost, you must evaluate to determine whether you are willing to pay the cost necessary to complete God's vision. In fulfilling His plan, like Abraham in Genesis 12, you may have to remove yourself from people you love. Like Apostle Paul in the book of Acts, you may have to sacrifice your personal plans to please the Lord.

Your family may have to pay a dear price. Are you willing to subject them to that? Can you endure the hardness necessary to complete the course? God demands more than just a monetary offering.

My baby daughter, Camari, died nearly 6 years ago at the time of this writing. It was a far more devastating incident than I realized. My entire family was traumatized! God did not tell me my daughter would die! I was **not** prepared for such a blow.

Understandably, many people have not been able to recover from child loss. I had to ask myself, "Am I willing and able to endure this pain and still complete God's plan for my life?"

My answer was and still is, "*YES*!"

Each of us must do a complete self-evaluation! Only *you* can determine if *you* will endure. And, I'm not telling you it was easy!

For years, I hated being around babies. In fact, I ***hated*** babies. I would not even hold one. When I saw fathers playing with their daughters in the park or eating an ice cream, I cried. I was broken but still preaching and leading ministry. I was determined to endure this pain and overcome it!

Don't get me wrong, I have a great son named Joshua. He is a brilliant young author himself. But since I had a son, all I wanted more than anything was a daughter. Camari's death went deep! It affected everyone in our church. My answer, though, was still, "**YES!**"

Today, I am able to enjoy babies all the time. God healed me from that tragedy because I chose not to let it define me. It cost a lot for me to overcome that pain, but I conquered it.

You can conquer any obstacle in front of you or pitfall in your past if you will merely trust God to strengthen you. This is where faith comes in big time. When your strength and courage are all gone, faith connects you to the strength of God. And His strength **never** fails.

Jesus said in the parable that men would mock those who do not finish the task they set out to build. If you have faith in God, even a tiny bit, you have more than enough to finish. This is not a race of quickness, it is a race of longevity and endurance. You may have paused or even slowed down, but don't quit. You only become a laughingstock if you throw in the towel.

PILLAR FIVE FINAL NOTE

About a month ago, I was at lunch with a good friend of mine, a very successful pastor. I have watched him and learned much from him over the last few years. During that lunch, he made a statement that I will never forget.

> *"The success you are trying to achieve now is going to be dependent on the relationships you develop over the next several years."*

I don't think many of us realize just how valuable relationships are. We abuse and take advantage of people. We neglect others until we need something from them. Or, we connect with people of wrong character because we have the wrong motives. The world teaches: *Bleed a relationship dry. And, once it no longer serves your needs, kill it!!*

This is not the way of God!

Relationships are valuable. People are filled with rich and vast reservoirs of knowledge, insight, experience, and resources. For the most part, they are more than willing to share their wealth with people who respect them.

In counting the cost of your life, goals, and desires, please, do not forget to calculate the people in your life and the relationships you have with them. Cherish them and treat them honorably. You never know when you will have to call on any one of them for wisdom, guidance, or a helping hand.

Your Jericho March To Excellence

1. **Have you counted the cost of all your hopes, dreams, and desires? Explain your situation.**

2. **How have you developed relationships in your Christian walk?**

3. **Are you prepared to allow God to finish what He has begun in you?**

4. **Do you believe God will strengthen you to endure to the end?**

5. **Follow the path of Nehemiah for the next 7 days. Journal about your experience here.**

PILLAR 6

The Spirit of Excellence

Excellence is an internal, spiritual reality which works its way through the soul of an individual and manifests externally. Seemingly, this is an unknown truth. The common misconception of excellence is that it is measured by outward signs.

Excellence is a spirit. Once it is firmly rooted in a person's life and supported by principles, it reveals itself to all by rewarding its possessor.

Daniel 5:11-14 *There is a man in thy kingdom, in whom is the spirit of the holy gods; and in the days of thy father light and understanding and wisdom, like the wisdom of the gods, was found in him; whom the king Nebuchadnezzar thy father, the king, I say, thy father, made master of the magicians, astrologers, Chaldeans, and soothsayers; [12] Forasmuch as an excellent spirit, and knowledge, and understanding, interpreting of dreams, and shewing of hard sentences, and dissolving of doubts, were found in the same Daniel, whom the king named Belteshazzar: now let Daniel be called, and he will shew the interpretation. [13] Then was Daniel brought in before the king. And the king spake and said unto Daniel, Art thou that Daniel, which art of the children of the captivity of Judah, whom the king my father brought out of Jewry? [14] I have even heard of thee, that the spirit of the gods is in thee, and that light and understanding and excellent wisdom is found in thee.*

Daniel 6:1-3 *It pleased Darius to set over the kingdom an hundred and twenty princes, which should be over the whole kingdom; [2] And over these three presidents; of whom Daniel was first: that the princes might give accounts unto them, and the king should have no damage. [3] Then this Daniel was preferred above the presidents and princes, because an excellent spirit was in him; and the king thought to set him over the whole realm.*

Some would say that Daniel was excellent because he received promotion. The truth, however, is that Daniel was promoted because he had an **excellent spirit**, something that distinguished him from all others. When there was trouble, leaders sought him out because he was recommended to them: his reputation preceded him. Daniel's reputation was one of excellence. As the above scriptures reveal, Daniel was offered to the King as a solution to his problem because of his excellent track record.

In Daniel Chapter 6, King Darius set up an infrastructure to effectively govern his kingdom, something in which he took great pleasure. It pleased Darius to install a team of 120 princes to govern various regions and states of the Persian Empire. Over these princes, he placed 3 presidents. The king then appointed Daniel as the chief of the presidents.

The princes had to answer to the presidents, the presidents

answered to Daniel, Daniel answered to the King. The Bible states that this *pleased* Darius. By placing Daniel over this governmental system, King Darius was protecting his investment.

Daniel was excellent because he served the King with no ulterior motives: there was no selfish agenda within him. He had no undermining political claims to fame. His focus was clear: make sure the King is protected! An excellent spirit is concerned with serving. Daniel served well.

First, he served the will of God. Then, he served the will of his King. There were several leadership and governmental changes during Daniel's life. Yet, through these transitions, Daniel remained constant. If he had personal feelings, he never voiced them. His impeccable history of faithfulness kept him in the presence and favor of the King.

During his time of service, Daniel interpreted dreams and supernatural phenomena. Even though it may have been bad news, he never lied to the King. Nor did he alter his words to make the king feel good. And, he was cherished for it.

Promotion is a byproduct of excellence. Excellent people are sought out by influential people for their wisdom. Anyone who has anything of worth wants to protect his or her possessions. An influential person will spare no expense in searching out excellent people to guide them in protecting their investments.

Daniel was much sought after because he possessed something all leaders need: excellence! And he was paid him well for that excellence! Each time he was called upon, he got richer. His excellent spirit rewarded him because excellence produces promotion.

What is Excellence?

Excellence: the fact or state of excelling; superiority; eminence.

Excellent: possessing outstanding quality or superior merit; remarkably good.

Excellence: to surpass or go beyond the normal standard to attain the highest level of eminence.

In school, a person who produces all "C's" is considered average. To me, this is astounding because the standard Grade Point Average (GPA) is based on a 4 point scale. A person with all "A's" earns a 4.0 GPA. A person with all "B's" earns a 3.0 GPA. The one with all "C's" earns a 2.0 GPA and a person with all "D's" earns a 1.0 GPA. Unfortunately, all "F's" means you get nothing.

Using this information, I can conclude that a "C" average, which society considers the normal performance level, is actually a failing grade. Simple math proves that half of 4 is 2. Translated to percents, 2/4 equals ½ or 50%. No matter what school you attend, nor what level of education you are at, 50% is always a failing grade: an "F." In other words, a "C" average is an "F"!

Because it is acceptable, many people are content with just being average. Average is failing, just getting by. Excellence can never be achieved through an average mindset. Just getting by can earn a diploma or even a college degree. Average people have jobs, they have families. However, they do not excel. To excel requires more than an average mindset and effort.

Average people won't excel because it means they will have to do hard work. The average person thinks within himself, *"Why should I do more when I can do ok like this?"* The average person is only willing to put forth enough effort to just get by.

On a physical training test, if five (5) pull-ups are the minimum to pass, the average minded person will ONLY do five. He will only perform the minimum requirements because he is perfectly content with average. He consoles himself by saying things like, *"At least I passed."*

Just making it is not excelling. To excel is to go beyond, to surpass, or exceed. Please don't misunderstand: there are some who excel *beyond* average. But, to excel is not excellence either.

A person achieving all "B's" is above average. This person exceeded the standard which is commendable. Yet, even a "B" average, a 3.0 GPA is only ¾ or 75%. This leaves a 25% range of potential increase! As long as there is room for improvement, we should strive for it wholeheartedly.

We don't want below average, average, or above average: we want excellence! Excellence is the state of eminence. Eminence is a place of great distinction or superiority. The "A" average, 4.0 GPA, represents this state of eminence and superiority: 100%. This represents perfection and completion of the highest rank.

As members of the Body of Christ, we have been chosen to dwell in this utmost elevation. Whether or not we actually achieve this position is solely up to us. God has already made excellence available to us. To accept any other way of life is an insult to God because He *is* excellent.

> Psalm 8:9 *O Lord our Lord, how excellent is Thy name in all the earth!*
>
> Psalm 148:13 *Let them praise the name of the Lord: for His name alone is excellent; His glory is above the earth and heaven.*
>
> Psalm 150:2 *Praise Him for His mighty acts: praise Him according to His excellent greatness.*

God is excellent! Everything He does is excellent. The scriptures above declare that God's name is excellent in all the earth. We, the people of God, are charged with keeping His name excellent in all the earth. We do this through faithfulness and diligence to His will. An average-minded individual cannot display excellence nor represent an excellent person.

Wealthy people do not hire average attorneys. Michael Jackson and O.J. Simpson both hired Johnny Cochran. Although he came with a premium price tag, he delivered what they wanted. His representative abilities were excellent. The late Mr. Cochran was able to convince a contaminated jury, contrary to popular opinion and media persuasion, to acquit two seemingly guilty individuals. That is a miracle!!

God paid a premium price for us. He expects us to represent him with excellence. When we live defeated lives, we lower the value of God's name. To settle for an average existence is not only beneath us, it is a misrepresentation of Him.

Since He is excellent, we must be excellent also. Whatever God is should be seen in us.

- Depression is not in God: it should not be in us.
- Disease is not in God: it should not be in us.
- Lying is not in God: it should not be in us.

Looking at us, the world sees the same mess on us that binds them: and they want nothing to do with God or us! Live up to the premium price paid for you! Pay the premium price of discipline and walk in excellence.

Humility

Proverbs 15:33 *The fear of the Lord is the instruction of wisdom; and before honour is humility.*
Proverbs 18:12 *Before destruction the heart of man is haughty, and before honour is humility.*
Proverbs 22:4 *By humility and the fear of the Lord are riches, and honour, and life.*
1 Peter 5:5 *Likewise, ye younger, submit yourselves unto the elder. Yea, all of you be subject one to another, and be clothed with humility: for God resisteth the proud, and giveth grace to the humble.*

Humility is a pillar of excellence. Because honor is a reward of excellence, we can easily conclude that if a person walks in excellence, he must possess humility. Humility, then, could be considered a prerequisite of honor. If God bestows honor on a person, it is certain that he walks in humility.

Excellence hinges on humility. Once humility is forsaken, excellence is immediately contaminated. It must be this way or

else the weight of the honor and promotion which excellence
attracts will crush a person unless properly supported by humility.
When this occurs, his excellent spirit is transformed into pride and
all that he gained is lost.

> Daniel 6:1-3   It *pleased Darius to set over the kingdom an*
> *hundred and twenty princes, which should be over the whole*
> *kingdom; [2] And over these three presidents; of whom Daniel*
> *was first: that the princes might give accounts unto them, and*
> *the king should have no damage. [3] Then this Daniel was*
> *preferred above the presidents and princes, because an*
> *excellent spirit was in him; and the king thought to set him*
> *over the whole realm.*

Once again, we examine Daniel. The Bible specifically states
that he possessed an excellent spirit. In fact, as you can clearly see,
verse 3 shares an even stronger point: he was preferred above his
contemporaries because of his excellent spirit. It was noticeable.
His spirit stood out more than his looks.

Daniel was originally chosen because he was handsome and
smart. Besides Daniel, there were several others, Shadrach,
Meshach, and Abednego, who were taken into captivity with
Daniel. The *average* chosen by the Babylonians were smart,
handsome young men. These four stood above average (handsome
and smart.) Daniel excelled above them all. He may have looked
appealing, but his spirit outshined his countenance, his wealth, and
his intellect.

Had Daniel not been full of humility, he would have been just
like everyone else. The other leaders were jealous of Daniel. They
all had political agendas and selfish ambitions and served the king
only to further their selfish appetites. They spent years vying for
power and jockeying for position. Daniel simply walked in
excellence and gained in moments what they tried to possess for
years.

No wonder they hated him! They lied, cheated, stole and moved slowly while Daniel was humble and meek and moving on the fast track.

Because of Daniel's excellence, the king gladly promoted him. But, it was his humility which sustained him. The King hand-selected certain people and placed them strategically in key positions so he would suffer no loss or damage.

When installing people in important positions, you must ensure they are of impeccable character because they will have the perfect opportunity to take advantage of you. The king knew he had to trust the ones he selected. So, as a precaution, he chose Daniel and gave him the coveted Chief President office. Conceivably, the King did this for two reasons:

1. He knew Daniel would not rob him.
2. He knew Daniel would hold his subordinates accountable to a system of excellence and would not allow them to rob the King either.

Daniel was humble. His heart was not set to take advantage of the King: his heart was set to serve and protect the King.

Humility is humble submission reinforced with meekness. Daniel's main focus was to prevent the King being robbed or blind-sided. He had charge of the entire Kingdom and its resources. Because he had no overseer besides the King, this was Daniel's truest character test.

Daniel knew the King trusted him. He also knew that the King was too busy to keep an eye on him at all times. He could have easily altered the books to reflect any reality he wanted. Instead, he walked in humility to honor the King. Daniel served faithfully without any regard for his personal wellbeing. His integrity brought much honor and respect to God.

Men praised God because of Daniel's humility and excellence. When we walk in humble excellence, we give glory to God, keeping His name excellent in all the earth.

The Humble Man...

- Seeks no personal gain
- Keeps his affairs in a godly manner
- Protects his leaders
- Allows God to honor and promote him
- Is careful to do and say only what pleases God
- Faithfully carries out His instructions
- Always looks within to ensure that his motives and intentions are pure

The Silence of Excellence

At first, walking in excellence seems very lonely because there is a silent period in which excellence matures within a person. There are two people in the scriptures who bare excellent spirits. We will examine them to clearly see how excellence is cultivated.

The men I speak of are Joseph and Daniel. These men are famous. They represent a breed of humanity which exemplifies strong character and supernatural prowess. Joseph and Daniel were free men who were enslaved.

Both rose to positions of great influence within their captive nations. Both men are the epitome of success: the antiquated equivalent of a *"rags to riches"* story.

There is no *"get-rich-quick scheme"* with these two. They spent a great deal of time in agonizing silence. Because of an excellent spirit within, though, they rose in favor regardless of their conditions. Whether slave or prisoner, they always found favor with those in authority.

Daniel found favor with the eunuch in charge of his care. Joseph found favor with both Potiphar and the Prison Chief. Yet, there is a noticeable reality which, because of the Bible's written format, often goes without attention: these men were essentially used by their captors for their excellence. Typically, after being used, they were sent back to silence.

There in obscurity, in the silence, excellence was cultivated in these men's lives on a greater scale. God would not allow them to get prideful. He used them, blessed them, and then, sent them back to silence.

The entire book of Daniel covers the life of this Prophet. During the first 6 chapters, Daniel ages decades. Daniel's life is a silent one. He is only called on in the most extreme cases. When he is summoned, he speaks very few words.

From a young age, Daniel was disciplined and focused. When offered the infamous *"King's meat,"* he refused to partake. He challenged his keepers to test him by giving him 10 days of pulse, beans. They reluctantly agreed to his terms.

Astonishingly, he fared better than all the others eating the King's meat. What everyone else considered the best, Daniel considered a defiling agent to decay his purity. He chose isolation and purity over popularity and pollution.

In silence, Daniel kept himself untainted by the filth of the Babylonian world. To be holy unto the Lord was his delight: he was content being isolated. Because he did not go along with their way of life, the Babylonians were indifferent to him and kept him in the background.

Although Daniel was considered to be a wise man, notice that the others did not consult with him on the interpretation of Nebuchadnezzar's dream. Other evidence of his wisdom is seen when the King ordered the death of all the wise men: they came to kill Daniel and his friends.

We know he was a wise man in their eyes and had influence with the king. When he requested more time from the King to hear from God so he could interpret his dream, his request was granted. As frustrated as the King was, he gave Daniel one more night. Daniel was thought to be wise, but he was not respected until this time.

Daniel spent some time seeking God to save his friends. He

boldly told the king he would tell and interpret his dream. Because of his tremendous relationship with God, Daniel was able to connect supernaturally to avert a life-threatening crisis. He came out of a silent place of obscurity to answer the King confidently.

Once he amazed and satisfied the king, Daniel was honored and God was glorified. Then, he was sent *back* into silence. Daniel is not heard from again until the King had another vision. Once again, Daniel represented God well. He was rewarded again. Then, back into silence again.

Then, when Belshazzar called on him at the word of his counselors, the same thing happened again. Daniel was constantly used, rewarded, and sent back to silence. It wasn't until Darius came to power that Daniel was truly honored and his prophetic gifting began to flourish.

His days of silence positioned Daniel and prepared him for each event that came his way. Threats of death, divine interpretations, governmental crisis, and enemy plots all attempted to destroy him, but Daniel was always prepared. He never worried because he did not despise his days of silence. In silence, God made him better. He drew closer to God and kept himself in a place of purity.

Unlike many people, Daniel showed no signs of frustration as a result of his silence. He seemed to relish his time with God.

So many people are not content in silent times: they want to move faster than God allows. Therefore, they become angered and agitated because their pride and egos are hurt.

They leave church. They stop seeking God, and refuse to walk in righteousness. They arrogantly believe they are punishing God.

"If You don't move," they say, "I'm going back into the world."

The blessing of God can't be high-jacked! The Spirit of Excellence must be cultivated in a private place. When God silences you, stay there and grow into maturity.

Joseph, on the other hand, is a bit different. He recognizes his greatness from childhood. Ignorantly, he voices it out loud. He is already hated by his brothers because his dad shows more favor to him than to them. Oblivious to his brother's feelings, he voices his dreams of greatness with reckless abandon.

His immaturity, coupled with his father's favor, expedited his trip to silence. His lack of humility caused him to endure an unpleasant 13-year season of humbleness. Though he suffered betrayal and loss, the excellent spirit within Joseph sustained him through slavery and prison all the way to Pharaoh's throne room.

Why such an extreme set of horrific circumstances? Because God intended to save a world struck with famine. He required a man of excellence tempered with humility to execute His will without stealing His glory. God wants His glory! People of excellence will ensure that the Lord gets every drop of it!

PILLAR SIX FINAL NOTE

Now, I am not a country boy. I was born and raised in the city of St. Louis. However, because my Grandmother is from southern Arkansas, I have had my fair share of country experiences growing up.

Every now and then, during those Arkansas trips, we would see frogs hop by and just sit. Now, because I wasn't a country boy, I would just look at them. But, my cousins (who were from the country) would gleefully chase them down, capture, and sometimes, slam those frogs to their death.

The smaller frogs were the hardest to catch. Again, I can't emphasize this enough: being from the city, I didn't bother getting my hands dirty with frogs. I could catch and clean fish and burn trash with the best of them. But, messing with frogs is where I drew the line. I just watched in amazement as my cousins tortured them.

The bigger (fatter) frogs, of course, were the easiest to catch. When I think of those frogs, I think about people who walk around with so much baggage in life. Fear and failure clog their minds and cloud their judgment.

These are people who lack excellence. They, like those fat frogs, are too heavy to escape those people in this world who cleverly await unsuspecting individuals to capture, torture, and destroy them. They are too heavy!!

Living in the past, being lazy, and passing off responsibility adds unwanted and unneeded fat to one's life. It makes a person heavy. And, though, like the fat frog who can jump, he is too inundated with fat to move swiftly enough to avoid the danger surrounding him.

Building an excellent spirit is just like shedding pounds in an exercise room and good dietary habits. It allows us to easily evade the destructive people who are all around us.

I watched my cousins torture many a frog in my life. I have

also seen a great number of people get hurt by things that did not have to hurt them if they had been more focused and disciplined. Let us shed the pounds of lazy and irresponsible living and quickly overcome all that seeks to harm us!

Your Jericho March To Excellence

1. What is your experience with times of silence?

2. What have you noticed most when you became silent before God?

3. How are you allowing God to cultivate the Spirit of Excellence within you?

4. In the Kingdom of God, are you maintaining your 4.0 (G.P.A. – God Pursuit Attitude)?

5. Follow the path of Daniel for the next 7 days. Journal about your experience here.

Adrian Taylor, Jr.

PILLAR 7

The Power of Explanation

Excuses, excuses, excuses...

Before we come to our conclusion, let's take some time to discuss the destructive nature of excuses.

Almost everyone uses excuses without knowing the full depth of their wickedness. Our post-modern society is in for a rude awakening, if you will, as it falls prey to the blatant disregard we have for being responsible.

In pride, we may proclaim to be responsible. However, the proof, as they say, rests firmly and irrefutably in the proverbial pudding. That pudding, of course, is the wretched nature of our pungent character.

Excuses are designed for only one thing: to remove or

alleviate a person from accepting responsibility. Somehow, we have determined that excuses are acceptable and valid. In addition, we have the nerve to get angry when someone does not accept our excuses.

Because excuses are deceptive, no one benefits from them. They project an appearance of innocence and maturity but hide a truer more grotesque reality. The one relying on excuses limps badly: he is wounded internally. The more excuses he uses, the greater the revelation of the severity of his inner dysfunction.

Excuses are typically offered when one is called into accountability. Accountability takes place when someone in authority requests that a subordinate give an account. The act of accountability demands that the subordinate submit and take responsibility for his actions… right or wrong.

If right, he will be rewarded with accolades or promotion. If wrong, he will have to suffer the consequences of his actions - reprimand or demotion. The acceptance of responsibility is golden. Whether right or wrong, the subordinate will grow.

I must bring clarification to two misconstrued terms: explanations and excuses. These two terms are very often highly mistaken for each other. They are distinct and must be clarified.

An **explanation** is the truthful presentation of events or actions which may have hindered an individual from fulfilling his or her obligations. An explanation is in no way a '*get out of jail free card!*' It merely serves as a **tool** of accountability.

The person who presents an explanation shows regard for his superiors and those he or she may have let down. He presents his explanation with the full understanding that there are still consequences he may have to face.

On the other hand, the one offering **excuses** presents a bland version of the truth. Typically, he is very evasive and must be cornered in order to find out what happened. Excuses are designed to remove a person from responsibility because he does not want to be accountable for his actions no matter how reckless they may be.

In short, people who present explanations seek no special treatment or amnesty. Those who offer excuses, however, seek justification and liberation from accountability. They want no reprimands, only sympathy for their failure.

The Problem with Excuses

People offering excuses often play the role of helpless victims who have no alternative but irresponsibility. People like this cannot be corrected or instructed because they perceive everything as a personal attack. They resent anyone who holds them accountable. They think everyone should understand their reasons for failing.

If you attempt to offer wisdom on how they could have done things differently or how they can avoid this occurrence in the future, they are offended. This is conspicuous rebellion! Unequivocally, this is pride.

In our church, we have a simple policy. I ask all leaders and workers to be upfront and communicate clearly. If you accept an assignment and for some reason are unable to fulfill it, please call the designated leader so your assignment can be covered by a suitable replacement. If you are going to be late, please contact us as soon as possible.

For example, if a greeter or usher is unable to make it to service for whatever reason - sick, family emergency, car break-down, tired, want to watch television, etc. - he or she should contact their immediate supervisor as soon as possible. If you wake up, get ready, and your car doesn't start at 9:15 a.m., you should not wait until 10:00 a.m. to call.

Also, if your car stops working the night before and you wait until the morning to report this, then, you are irresponsible. You could have arranged for a ride. Or, if you must miss, call your supervisor so your post can be adequately covered. The only acceptable reason for not calling is if some strange instance occurs in which you are caught in an unforeseen circumstance where no phone is readily available.

This may seem insensitive. But, if people treated their jobs the way they treat God's house, the unemployment rate would skyrocket above 77% overnight. Your employer does not care whether your car breaks down or if you are sick. If you do not act responsibly, they replace you.

An employer's profits are affected when you do not communicate. More importantly, God's integrity is undermined when you do not fulfill your obligations to Him. This is irresponsible behavior.

Excuses are faulty crutches for lazy, irresponsible people. They are the quick, easy fix no one accepts but the one who uses them.

If you commit to helping your friend redo her resume, then, you need to do so. To skip out on that commitment is irresponsible and disrespectful. Calling her later to say, "*something came up,*" is pure ignorance. She honored you by believing that your words were valuable, she was repaid through your betrayal.

As a result, just like a rubber check, your word and lifestyle are now marked with a huge red "**NSF.**" The funny thing, though, is that *you* have the nerve to be upset with **her** for getting angry. She has the right to do so! Not only did you stand her up, you also didn't call her and refused to own up to your failure by giving her a *lame* excuse!

When depending on excuses, you will never find solutions. Because excuse givers are unstable, it causes them to exhibit irresponsible behavior.

If you have school work or pressing chores, they should be completed in a timely manner. They should never be the cause for not fulfilling your obligations. Many people claim tiredness or exhaustion. This, too, is not valid because people make time for what is important to them.

An alcoholic transient claims to never have enough money yet always has a bottle in his hand. A crack addict always finds ways to get high. An intercessor always finds time to pray. Being busy does not validate an excuse because you have the time to adjust. The solution is simple: **sacrifice**!

Use your time wisely. Carve out study time for school. Set aside time to do your housework. Stop infringing on the time you have committed to others. Excuses are a branch from selfishness. The excuse user will not dare inconvenience himself. But, he has no reservations at all about robbing others for self satisfaction.

This instability is evidence of a serious default: double-mindedness! The scriptures declare that *a double-minded man is unstable in all his ways* (James 1:8). Everything he does is unstable, there is no consistency. Nothing can be accomplished with unstable people. The reason they always offer excuses is because they are drowning in their own instability.

They may *want* to be committed but experience only chaos. Because God does not readily move for them, they think they are victims of the devil. Instead, they are unfortunate victims of their own double-mindedness. When they ask God for things, they get nothing because they are double-minded.

Instability is easily recognizable when a person experiences constant turmoil: frequent moves from place to place, going from church to church, phone numbers always changing, freak problems, and emergencies continually impede progress. A person perpetuates this lifestyle by offering excuses and shunning responsibility.

Fearful that people will learn how unstable they really are, they hide behind excuses, not realizing they are fooling no one. If there is always some sort of emergency or problem, there is certain to be instability.

Excuses are Signs of Deeper Problems

- Excuses cause contempt
- Excuses are the calling card of the foolish
- Excuses attempt to hide instability
- Excuses provide ample opportunity for chaos to lurk
- Excuses seek to hide pain and depression
- Excuses are the faulty crutch of the lazy

CHAPTER SEVEN FINAL NOTE

I was at breakfast today with a very wise man of God, Apostle William Bird. One of my habits of excellence is to have lunch or breakfast with very wise and disciplined people of influence who can keep my mind sharp and focused. I do this quite frequently.

While talking, he shared with me a clear word from God that came to him a few weeks back when he was in a hotel room. He said the Lord revealed to him…

"You will never know breakthrough until you learn the difference between boundaries and barriers."

Wow!

That was an amazing concept to me. Both barriers and boundaries are causes for why so many people use excuses. A barrier is typically a hindrance of some sort, things we may need to overcome in order to advance.

I-70 runs through the city of Denver. However, just west of the city stands the Rocky Mountains. At one point when building I-70, those mountains were a barrier. Engineers and construction crews had to strategize to overcome those mountains. With great planning, skill, and effort, they built a winding road through a geographical behemoth.

They could have used excuses that the mountains were too high and some of those hills were solid iron. Instead, they canned the excuses and plowed a highway. Now, millions travel across the Rocky Mountains every year. Barriers are made to be overcome with hard work and good planning.

Boundaries, on the other hand, are for safety and protection. A backyard fence provides safety for children and pets. It also keeps out unwanted dangers. A fence is not designed to impede one's progress. On the contrary, it serves as a sign that potential danger lies beyond this point: **Proceed with caution**.

Curbs and sidewalks tell us the same thing. They are not designed to hinder us. Instead, they indicate that we are entering into a new environment and must stay alert from this point forward.

Think about it. When one reaches an intersection after walking on the sidewalk, the curb tells him to "*look both ways*" before you cross into the street. The street itself is not inherently dangerous. But, because the street is where automobiles travel, there is an increased potential for more danger if one is not focused.

Boundaries and barriers can both be impediments if we do not have the right knowledge. However, once we are mature and throw away excuses, there is no obstacle which can block our forward progress.

Your Jericho March To Excellence

1. **What excuses do you see yourself constantly using that impede your progress?**

2. **How often have you used these excuses?**

3. **How can you allow God to change the way you use excuses?**

4. **What excuse are you going to abolish from your life right now?**

5. **Create a NO EXCUSE zone in your life. Journal about your experience here.**

Adrian Taylor, Jr.

CONCLUSION

Proverbs 17:27 *He that hath knowledge spareth his words: and a man of understanding is of an excellent spirit.*
Proverbs 22:20 *Have not I written to thee excellent things in counsels and knowledge…*

God has '*written*' excellent things to and for us. In other words, the written Word of God, the Bible, overflows with the knowledge and counsel of excellence. If one desires to be excellent, he need only give himself over to the study and implementation of the Bible. As he gains an understanding, the scripture above reads, his excellent spirit is revealed.

The bottom line is this: diligent Bible study plus a strong understanding of scripture produces an excellent spirit.

```
Diligent Bible Study
+
Strong Understanding
=
Excellent Spirit
```

The principles I have outlined for you in *Pillars of Excellence* are all concepts taught to us from the Bible.

The House of Excellence

In construction, a proper foundation is the key to a solid structure. Fortunately for us, the foundation has already been set. God has laid Jesus as the foundation for our lives. I Corinthians 3 strongly urges us to be careful how we build on that foundation.

For the sake of this conversation, excellence serves as the roof. Like a roof, excellence is heavy but covers and protects everyone underneath. If it is raining or snowing, a well-built roof prevents water from touching or damaging anyone inside.

Excellence keeps the evil intentions of evil adversaries from affecting our lives. However, like a roof, excellence must also be supported. That is where the *pillars* or principles in this book come into play. We abide under the mercy and grace of an excellent life when we install the necessary principles in our lives.

Each principle is a pillar which keeps excellence hoisted high over us. I urge you to go back and review all of the ideas of this book over and over. They are not suggestions from a man: they are God's simple instructions to us. Following them will vastly improve our focus and way of life.

Installing these divine principles will be time-consuming. Like any good skill, they require time, effort, and energy to master. Houses are not built over night, neither is a life of excellence. Install each principle with care and keep good watch over it to ensure it stays strong.

All things require maintenance or will soon deteriorate. And please, do not substitute a lesser material! There is no substitute for God's Word! Eve tried that in the garden and look where that has gotten us! Invest the time and resources necessary to properly install God's blessed principles in your life.

Excellence is God's perfect design for you! So, walk in it!

The Whole Matter

Solomon writes in Ecclesiastes 12:13 that we should hear the conclusion of the whole matter. In his great dissertation, he based his conclusion on two main ideas:
1. Fear God
2. Keep His commandments

Solomon stated that these two principles were the *"whole duty of man."* Consequently, God, the writer further remarked, was going to judge mankind for everything public and private. Since God is going to be so thorough in His examination of His creation, it behooves us to understand how to live a life that is pleasing to Him.

An excellent spirit demonstrates a person's fear of God. Through his life, he says that he trusts and honors God. The person with an excellent spirit has developed enough character to be humble and allow God to bless him. He will not take short cuts and will not defile himself with anything not approved by God. This is the life we have all been ordained for and called to.

Every year in Denver, an event known as *"The Parade of Homes"* is held. During this time, a high-class neighborhood full of beautiful homes is chosen. People are charged admission to tour these houses for several days. My wife and I went one year. Certainly, these houses did not disappoint in their style and grandeur. Each house was progressively more exquisite than the previous one.

As we walked through these uniquely designed homes with

architectural details that could rival some of history's most prized creations, we heard the remarks of others on the tour.

"This is gorgeous!"

"I would love to live in a house like this!"

Then, there were some who said things like, *"My God, I like this house! But, I ain't paying this much money to live here!"*

You see, excellence is just like those houses: beautiful, admirable, unique and many people want to tour it. They just don't want to pay for it! To them, it is too expensive. They are right! The cost of excellence is very high but well worth it.

Pay the price for an excellent life. The blessing of the Lord will abide in you and God will receive all the glory. That is the whole duty of man... to be **EXCELLENT**!

Adrian Taylor, Jr.
The Apostle of Truth

ABOUT THE AUTHOR

Adrian Taylor, Jr. was born and raised in St. Louis, Missouri. Living in the inner-city, Adrian learned very quickly that he had *precocious* communication and leadership skills. That's a fancy way of saying he talked too much and couldn't sit still. Adrian went to Southern Illinois University - Edwardsville, where he studied Speech Communications. It was there he met his beloved wife, LaKenya, whom he married in January 2000. The newlyweds moved to Denver a year later.

In October of 2003, Adrian founded Lighthouse Church International in Aurora, Colorado, with 4 people in his living room. The church quickly grew and many began attending. After 9 years, in response to taking over as Pastor of a struggling congregation, Adrian and his family relocated to Cape Girardeau, MO where they restructured the church and founded Lighthouse Breakthrough International Ministries. For 4 years, he has transformed a fledgling, hurting congregation into a healthy thriving place of victory and peace.

Adrian Taylor, Jr. is an Ordained, Internationally recognized Apostle and Pastor. He is affiliated with United Christian Church of Gadsden, Alabama where he serves as the International Missions Director for Vertical Apostolic Covering - an association of independent, non-denominational churches. He has recently been appointed as the Vice-Chief Apostle of the newly formed *Coalition of Interdependent Apostles* based in Cape Girardeau, MO. He is also a board member of the Business Research Institute in Sikeston, MO and holds a Bachelor's Degree in Theology from Covenant Bible College and Seminary where he is currently completing his Master's Degree in Biblical Counseling.

Adrian is a highly sought-after author and speaker. He is dynamic and energetic in his presentation and has a unique approach to the Bible that allows people of all walks to connect with him and clearly understand complex ideas. He has traveled globally sharing the good news of Jesus Christ and hopes to continue the faithful work of the Lord by building bridges and making strategic alliances that will impact lives for God and leave a valuable legacy for generations to come.

Adrian and LaKenya are the proud parents of Joshua, a 13-year old genius who has authored 2 published books and plans to attend Mizzou and study Journalism.

Adrian Taylor, Jr.

If your group would like to purchase this and other books by Adrian Taylor, Jr. in bulk, please contact us at http://drillsergeantoflife.com/heard-word-publishing/.

If you would like to engage Adrian Taylor, Jr, *The Apostle of Truth,* to speak at your conference or event, please contact him at 720-271-7478 or ApostleATJ@gmail.com.

CHECK YOUR LEADING BOOKSTORE OR ORDER HERE

- ☐ YES, I want _____ copies of *Pillars of Excellence* at $18.00 each, plus $5 shipping per book. Canadian orders must be accompanied by a postal money order in U.S. funds. Allow 15 days for delivery.
- ☐ I also want _____ copies of *Faith Focus* at $15.00 each, plus $5 shipping per book. Canadian orders must be accompanied by a postal money order in U.S. funds. Allow 15 days for delivery.

My check or money order for $_____ is enclosed.
Please charge my Visa _____, MasterCard _____, Discover _____ or American Express _____.

Name _____

Organization _____

Address _____

City/State/Zip _____

Phone _____ Email _____

Card # _____ Exp. Date _____

Signature _____

Please make check payable and return to:

Heard Word Publishing

1980 Van Buren Way

Aurora, CO 80011

www.ingramcontent.com/pod-product-compliance
Lightning Source LLC
Chambersburg PA
CBHW070516090426
42735CB00012B/2809